EMERGENCY PLANNING

FOR JUVENILE JUSTICE RESIDENTIAL FACILITIES

Office of Juvenile Justice and Delinquency Prevention

October 2011

U.S. Department of Justice
Office of Justice Programs
810 Seventh Street NW.
Washington, DC 20531

Eric H. Holder, Jr.
Attorney General

Laurie O. Robinson
Assistant Attorney General

Jeff Slowikowski
Acting Administrator
Office of Juvenile Justice and Delinquency Prevention

Office of Justice Programs
Innovation • Partnerships • Safer Neighborhoods
www.ojp.usdoj.gov

Office of Juvenile Justice and Delinquency Prevention
ojjdp.gov

Cover photos: FEMA/Andrea Booher (top photo), FEMA/Jocelyn Augustino (bottom photo).

The Office of Juvenile Justice and Delinquency Prevention is a component of the Office of Justice Programs, which also includes the Bureau of Justice Assistance; the Bureau of Justice Statistics; the National Institute of Justice; the Office for Victims of Crime; and the Office of Sex Offender Sentencing, Monitoring, Apprehending, Registering, and Tracking.

Foreword

We are pleased to offer this document to guide juvenile justice residential facilities in preparing for, responding to, and recovering from emergencies. *Emergency Planning for Juvenile Justice Residential Facilities* is the first comprehensive planning guide to address the specific needs of children, youth, and families involved in the justice system during an emergency.

The document was developed in response to the National Commission on Children and Disasters' recommendation in October 2009 that the Office of Juvenile Justice and Delinquency Prevention (OJJDP) conduct an assessment of emergency preparedness among state, county, and local juvenile justice systems. OJJDP found that the plans they examined were predominately intended for basic continuity of operations rather than comprehensive emergency planning, response, and recovery.

The Commission also recommended that OJJDP form a working group whose mission is to improve juvenile justice emergency preparedness nationwide. In response, OJJDP established the Justice Working Group on Children and Disasters, which comprises staff from federal agencies, experts in emergency planning, juvenile justice practitioners, mental and behavioral health professionals, and educators, many of whom administered programs or were first responders in a major emergency during the past 5 years. For months, the working group members met to share resources and experiences in the area of emergency planning, response, and recovery. *Emergency Planning for Juvenile Justice Residential Facilities* is the result of their work.

Through the guidance offered in this document, we encourage facilities to develop comprehensive emergency plans that will make a real and tangible difference in the safety and well-being of the most vulnerable individuals in our nation's justice system. These young people, their families, and the staff who care for them deserve nothing less.

Laurie O. Robinson
Assistant Attorney General
Office of Justice Programs

Acknowledgments

A special debt of gratitude is owed to Melodee Hanes, lead coordinator of the Justice Working Group on Children and Disasters, who was the guiding force behind this project. Her enthusiasm and commitment were critical to the team effort and to keeping the project on track.

We would also like to express our thanks to the Justice Working Group's Simon Gonsoulin and Christopher Bruno, who provided most of the content for this document. Their firsthand knowledge about juvenile justice residential facilities and their experiences in emergency response and recovery were indispensable to the project.

Many thanks also go to the Office of Juvenile Justice and Delinquency Prevention's (OJJDP's) Scott Pestridge, who served as the liaison between the Office and the Justice Working Group; and to Randall Gnatt of the National Commission on Children and Disasters, who provided sound advice at every step in the process.

Christine Tansey of Lockheed Martin Information Systems and Global Solutions, who served as editorial manager, was instrumental in seeing the document through from the draft stage to its final form.

Acknowledgments also are due to the Federal Emergency Management Agency's (FEMA's) Donald Lumpkins, who offered his expertise in the development of emergency operations plans and provided many helpful suggestions.

Any project of this scope entails the cooperation of many individuals, and thanks go to the entire Justice Working Group. Their reviews of the document were pivotal to ensuring its accuracy and completeness. Following is a list of the group's members:

Lead Coordinator

Melodee Hanes, J.D.
Deputy Administrator for Policy
OJJDP
Office of Justice Programs

Members

Susan James-Andrews, M.S.
Juvenile Justice Consultant
James-Andrews & Associates
Challenges

Paulette Aniskoff
Chair
Children's Working Group
FEMA

Valerie Boykin
Juvenile Justice Consultant

Christopher Bruno
Supervisor
Rivarde Detention Center
Jefferson Parish, LA

Howard Davidson, J.D.
Director
Center on Children and the Law
American Bar Association

Daniel Dodgen, Ph.D.
Director
Office for At-Risk Individuals
Behavioral Health and Human
    Services Coordination
Office of the Assistant Secretary
    for Preparedness & Response
Office of the Secretary
U.S. Department of Health and
    Human Services

Randall Gnatt, J.D.
Policy Director
National Commission on Children
    and Disasters (NCCD)

Simon G. Gonsoulin, M.Ed.
Principal Research Analyst and
    Juvenile Justice Resource
    Specialist
American Institutes for Research

Kathi Grasso, J.D.
Senior Juvenile Justice Policy
    and Legal Advisor
OJJDP

Judge Ernestine S. Gray, J.D.
Chief Judge
Orleans Parish Juvenile Court
New Orleans, LA

Heather King
Supervisory Program Manager
Planning and Assistance Branch
National Preparedness Directorate
FEMA

Lauralee Koziol
Lead Coordinator
Children's Working Group
FEMA

Dave Kuker
Juvenile Justice Specialist
Iowa Division of Criminal &
    Juvenile Justice Planning

Bruce Lockwood, C.E.M.
Commissioner
NCCD
Public Health Emergency
    Response Coordinator
Bristol-Burlington Health
    District, CT

Ned Loughran
Executive Director
Council of Juvenile Correctional
    Administrators

Donald Lumpkins, J.D.
Chief
Planning and Assistance Branch
National Preparedness Directorate
FEMA

Roland Mertz
Director
Bureau of Community
    Preparedness
Pennsylvania Emergency
    Management Agency (PEMA)

Jim Messinger
Emergency Management
    Specialist
PEMA

William Modzeleski, M.P.A.
Associate Assistant Deputy
    Secretary
U.S. Department of Education

Lisa Portune, M.S.W., L.I.S.W.
Juvenile Court Consultant

Christopher J. Revere, M.P.A.
Executive Director
NCCD

Zoe Savitsky
OJJDP Intern (summer 2010)

Gregory A. Thomas, M.S.
Emergency Preparedness
    Consultant
The Alan Thomas Security
    Group LLC

Tracy Wareing, J.D.
(Former) Counselor to
    the Secretary
U.S. Department of Homeland
    Security

Table of Contents

Introduction

Wildfires, floods, hazardous material spills, hurricanes, earthquakes, and tornadoes—emergencies[1] can strike anytime, anywhere. In fact, the number of annual federal disaster declarations has more than doubled over the past few decades. All juvenile justice residential facilities[2] need plans to prepare for, respond to, and recover from these emergencies so that the essential services they provide can become operational again as soon as possible after an emergency strikes. Emergency planning for these facilities takes on even greater significance because children are often the most vulnerable population in disasters, and protecting them from physical harm and trauma is essential.

Emergency Planning for Juvenile Justice Residential Facilities provides information about how facilities can ensure that youth receive the supports and services they require as they experience the disruptions that emergencies inevitably cause. This document emphasizes the importance of ongoing communication and collaboration with community partners in the emergency planning process. In addition, facilities are encouraged to prepare for all emergencies that may affect their geographical area—for everything from a fire in a building to a major flood, earthquake, or hurricane that impacts the surrounding region.

The emergency management cycle encompasses four interdependent phases: prevention/mitigation,[3] preparedness, response, and recovery. Prevention/

mitigation measures create a safer environment and facilitate recovery from later emergencies by reducing the risk of serious damage. Preparedness in the form of drills and exercises helps ensure an effective and efficient emergency response. During the recovery phase, careful assessments of what worked and what did not contribute to improved preparedness for subsequent emergencies. All phases are vital elements in the emergency management cycle.

This publication provides key principles and recommendations, but it is not overly prescriptive. Emergency planners inevitably will need to adapt these guidelines to the particular requirements of their facilities. This document is targeted to state, county, and local juvenile justice authorities charged with the custodial care and supervision of youth in the juvenile justice system, with particular focus on those authorities who oversee residential treatment and correctional and detention facilities that house juveniles via court-ordered placements. The principles outlined in this document may also apply to emergency planning for youth in out-of-home placement.

The document is divided into 12 sections. Section 1 provides an overview of the planning process and provides information about forming a planning team; assessing the facility's preparedness; analyzing courses of action; and writing, approving, disseminating, exercising, and updating the plan. Sections 2–12 provide an indepth look at key issues juvenile justice

---

[1] For the purposes of this document, "emergency" means an incident—natural, technological, or manmade—that requires a response to protect life, property, or the environment. In addition to the examples just provided, emergencies may include extreme heat and cold, tsunamis, landslides, terrorist threats, civil unrest, nuclear accidents, aircraft accidents, war-related disasters, utility failures, hostage crises, sexual assaults, bomb threats, and public health and medical emergencies.

[2] In this document, the term "juvenile justice residential facility" is defined as any secure-care or detention facility designed to confine youth for either the short or long term. The facility may be operated by state, county, local, or private entities.

[3] Mitigation refers to activities that are designed to reduce the loss of life and property as a result of serious emergencies by lessening the impact of the disaster and creating a safer environment. These activities, which generally have a long-term and sustained effect, help fix the cycle of damage, reconstruction, and repeated damage (Federal Emergency Management Agency, 2010).

residential facilities may want to consider as they write or update their plans. These issues include emergency preparedness training for staff; the protection of critical infrastructure; protocols for communication with families,[4] other agencies, and the public; and effective emergency medical care and mental health services. An extensive list of references and resources at the end of the document provides additional sources of information about how to best prepare for, respond to, and recover from emergencies.

Through its step-by-step guidance in the planning process, *Emergency Planning for Juvenile Justice Residential Facilities* will help ensure the efficient continuation of operations during an emergency, the reduction of risk to the physical plant, and, most importantly, the safety and well-being of youth and staff in our nation's juvenile justice residential facilities.

---

[4] The term "families" encompasses all primary caretakers of youth, including biological family members, guardians, foster parents, etc.

Section 1: Overview of the Planning Process

Juvenile justice residential facilities are charged with the responsibility of safely detaining youth while providing them with the academic programs, medical and mental health treatment, and life skills and vocational training they so urgently need. There are more than 2,400 residential facilities in the United States, which house more than 81,000 juvenile offenders (Hockenberry, Sickmund, and Sladky, 2011). Emergency planning for these facilities requires a special set of considerations that involve collaborative efforts across the spectrum—emergency management experts, administrators of state secure-care facilities and local detention facilities, juvenile court officials, law enforcement personnel, child welfare professionals, and medical and mental health personnel.

Many youth in residential placement have a history of trauma and exposure to violence and are particularly vulnerable to the aftereffects of a major emergency. Caring for their needs, as well as the needs of the staff who work at residential facilities—usually under demanding circumstances and in a stressful environment—requires advance planning. A comprehensive emergency plan, which prepares for a range of emergencies and involves many stakeholders in the community across a range of disciplines, will help ensure the safety and well-being of youth and also will enable staff to carry out their responsibilities as effectively and efficiently as possible during an emergency.

Emergency preparedness is a continuous cycle of planning, organizing, equipping, training, exercising, evaluating, and taking corrective action (see figure below). These activities are part of an ongoing cycle of improvement as planners analyze the effectiveness of the facility's response to recent emergencies and make appropriate adjustments to enhance the management of subsequent emergencies. All emergency operations plans (EOPs) are living documents; they change as new knowledge is gained and as the situations that planners face develop and evolve.

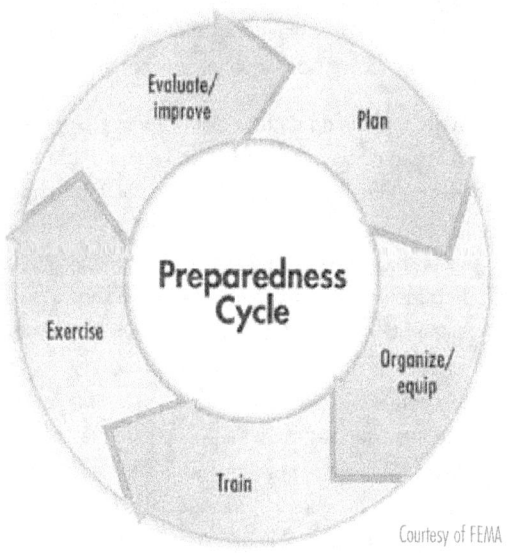

Courtesy of FEMA

Following are basic guidelines for planning:

- **Adopt an "all-hazards" approach.** Juvenile justice residential facilities should be prepared for the full range of emergencies that can occur on their premises and in the surrounding area. This "all-hazards" approach ensures the best possible preparation for these contingencies, which may involve quite different activities in the response phase.

Important Tips for Emergency Planning

- Adopt an "all-hazards" approach.
- Collaborate with partners and stakeholders.
- Establish a chain of command.
- Write a planning document.
- Exercise, review, and revise the plan.

- **Collaborate with partners and stakeholders.** Planning is most effective when it is coordinated with federal, state, county, and local juvenile justice agencies as well as with the state's emergency management agency, law enforcement, the courts, emergency medical services (EMS), human services, public health, fire, and public works departments, to name a few. The effectiveness of a response to an emergency depends on close cooperation and teamwork and a clear delineation of roles and responsibilities.

- **Establish a chain of command.** Developing an organizational structure—also known as an Incident Command System (ICS)—for managing the emergency brings order and stability to the facility's staff and residents, as well as to the surrounding community. This standardized approach integrates the functions of facilities, equipment, procedures, and communications. The ICS should be directly tied to the state, county, and local emergency systems.

- **Write a planning document.** Emergency preparedness should have at its center a written document that provides a tangible reference point for planners and staff. The document should contain a detailed breakdown of emergencies that could occur in a facility's geographical area (also known as a vulnerability assessment) and guidelines for every facet of emergency response and recovery, including communications with families of youth, youth-serving agencies, and the public; the roles and responsibilities of staff; procedures for sheltering in place and evacuation; arrangements for emergency medical and mental health services; and the measures in place for meeting the short- and long-term needs of residents and staff.

- **Exercise, review, and revise the plan.** Staff should be trained to respond to an emergency through regular drills. The plan should be reviewed and revised if areas that require improvement are identified. At a minimum, the plan should be reviewed

FEMA/Jocelyn Augustino

and updated once a year. Plans should evolve as lessons are learned, new information and insights become available, and priorities change.

Forming a Planning Team

Experience has demonstrated conclusively that emergency planning is best done by a team. This coordination clarifies roles and responsibilities at all levels. Planners at the juvenile justice residential facility should solicit information from staff about how operations under their purview may be affected by the emergencies likely to occur in their geographical area. Staff from every major department should be consulted about the challenges emergencies pose to continuity of operations. Their observations and recommendations should be discussed and incorporated into the EOP.

FEMA/Mark Wolfe

Recommended Participants in the Planning Process

A juvenile justice residential facility's planning team should include key staff from the following departments:

- Administration.
- Security.
- Maintenance.
- Finance/accounting.
- Human resources.
- Information technology.
- Programming (medical, mental health, academic, and recreation programs).

Planning team members from the larger community should include:

- Juvenile justice agency representatives.*
- Emergency management officials.
- Juvenile and family court administrators.
- Probation officers.
- Prosecutors and defense attorneys.
- Child welfare agency administrators.
- Public health professionals.
- Law enforcement and fire department officials.
- Medical and mental health experts.
- Emergency medical services providers.
- Mental health professionals.
- Education partners.
- Public works agencies (e.g., water, electricity, and garbage-removal services).
- Current contract service providers (e.g., transportation companies, medical and mental health contractors, food services).
- Members of nonprofit organizations (e.g., community-based mental health providers, faith-based programs, the YMCA).
- Families and youth involved with the juvenile justice system.
- Youth advocates.
- Volunteers.

FEMA/Manny Broussard

*In this document, "juvenile justice agency" refers to the agency that oversees juvenile justice residential facilities in a given region or state. Representatives of the juvenile justice agency are critically important members of the planning team because they can help to ensure that emergency policies, procedures, and plans developed by these facilities are aligned with each other as well as with those of higher governing authorities (e.g., the governor's office). This alignment is essential to an efficient use of resources and a coordinated approach to emergency planning.

The facility's emergency planning must be coordinated with planning efforts at the state, county, and local levels. An Office of Juvenile Justice and Delinquency Prevention-supported study (Andrews and Yeres, 2006) conducted in the aftermath of Hurricane Katrina found that juvenile justice systems that responded most effectively to the storms were active participants in a broad-based planning team with a history of collaboration.

The shared knowledge and cooperation of this multidisciplinary team will help ensure the development of a comprehensive and coordinated EOP. In addition, a collaborative approach often contributes to the development of creative and innovative strategies for coping with an emergency.

An example of collaboration between stakeholders might be an agreement with law enforcement agencies during the planning phase to assist in transporting adjudicated youth across multiple county lines during an evacuation. A police escort has the added benefit of ensuring the efficient and safe movement of youth through cities and evacuation routes immediately preceding or following a disaster. Another example might be the signing of memorandums of understanding (MOUs) with potential host centers in neighboring states to move youth across county or state lines in the event that an evacuation becomes necessary. Issues such as staffing, reimbursement, housing for youth and staff, and the provision of services are among the issues that might be addressed in the MOUs.

A high-ranking official from a state, county, or local emergency management agency should review the facility's EOP if agency representatives are unable to serve on the planning team. The official should provide feedback about the thoroughness of the plan; about improvements needed in the plan to maintain the safety of youth, staff, and the public; and about whether the plan is appropriately aligned with EOPs at the state, county, and local levels.

Agreements with the courts, child welfare agencies, and other youth-serving agencies regarding procedures for evacuation in an emergency should be developed during the planning process and kept on file. Agreements with the juvenile courts should specify the circumstances under which nonviolent offenders can be released to their families in the event of an evacuation and the procedures for the release.

Conducting a Vulnerability Assessment

Before an EOP is written, a vulnerability assessment should be conducted to determine which emergencies a facility is at greatest risk of experiencing. This research will help determine the threats that merit special attention in planning. Planners should gather information about the potential hazards, available resources, and geographic or topological characteristics that could affect emergency operations. The results of the vulnerability assessment will serve as an indispensable guide in the shaping of the emergency plan.

Planners should consider working with state, county, and local emergency management and law enforcement to assess the hazards faced by their facility and

NOAA News Photo

to determine how these threats might influence planning efforts. Vulnerability assessments should have already been completed by the emergency management agencies, and these agencies may be able to provide valuable information and to help prevent duplication of effort. Reviewing the emergency plans and policies of other juvenile justice residential facilities also can serve as a helpful starting point in writing a plan.

Identifying Essential Functions

Once the vulnerability assessment has been conducted, planners should identify all functions of the facility and then determine the ones that must be continued under all circumstances. These essential functions should be prioritized, and the staffing and resources required to keep them in operation should be specified. In addition, planners should identify supporting activities that ensure that essential functions continue to be carried out during and following an emergency.

If a written document already exists, planners should consult with the facility's key staff to gain feedback on the problems they encountered the last time the EOP was implemented, either through a drill or a response to an actual emergency. This task will help planners to identify gaps in the plan and make appropriate adjustments. In addition, the facility's policies should be assessed to determine whether they are consistent with an all-hazards approach.

Determining Goals and Objectives

Once a planning team has been formed and the vulnerability assessment has been completed, the process of developing goals and objectives can begin. Planners should allow the results and findings of these preliminary activities to help shape the facility's goals and objectives.

Goals are general statements that provide an overview of what emergency operations are designed to accomplish. Objectives outline the major elements of a plan that will enable the facility to realize the goals it has set. The EOP lays out how the objectives will be realized through specific activities and procedures. In the days and weeks following an emergency, the objectives will provide an important measure of the effectiveness of the facility's response and recovery efforts.

Developing and Analyzing Courses of Action, Identifying Resources

During this step, planners develop and compare possible solutions for achieving the goals and objectives identified in the previous step. This planning should include a sequenced structure for responding to and recovering from an emergency and for facilitating long-term operations during a major emergency. The planning team might consider working through this process by using charts or timelines that help members visualize response flow.

Writing the Plan

The written plan constitutes a blueprint for action in responding to an emergency. Following is an overview of a possible structure for an EOP. The overview is based on one of the most widely used formats for EOPs, commonly known as the traditional functional format. It consists of three sections: the basic plan, functional annexes, and hazard-specific annexes.[5] The basic plan provides a general overview of information relevant to the EOP, whereas the annexes focus on specific responsibilities, tasks, and actions required to successfully implement the EOP. It should be noted that the following summary is for general guidance purposes only. The structure of the EOP should be adjusted as necessary to meet the individual needs and requirements of each juvenile justice residential facility.

Basic Plan

Promulgation Statement. Announces the plan, gives it official status, and grants authority and responsibility to carry out the tasks.

Record of Changes. Presents in chronological order all of the updates or changes to the plan, the section of the EOP affected by the change, the date of the change, and the individual who made the change (see Sample Record of Changes Form on page 8).[6]

Record of Distribution. Can be used to prove that relevant individuals have received, reviewed, and accepted the plan. Usually includes the date of delivery, number of copies received, method of delivery, and recipient's name and title. This form generally uses a table format similar to the Sample Record of Changes Form.

---

[5] The summary of the components of the basic plan, functional annexes, and hazard-specific annexes has been adapted with permission from FEMA's *Developing and Maintaining Emergency Operations Plans: Comprehensive Preparedness Guide 101, Version 2.0* (2010), pp. 3-12 through 3-18, available at fema.gov/pdf/about/divisions/npd/CPG_101_V2.pdf.

[6] The Sample Record of Changes Form is taken with permission from FEMA's *Continuity of Operations Plan Template for Federal Departments and Agencies* (n.d.), p. 6, available at fema.gov/pdf/about/org/ncp/coop/continuity_plan_template.pdf.

Sample Record of Changes Form

Change Number	Section of EOP	Date of Change	Individual Making Change	Description of Change
1.				
2.				
3.				

Purpose, Scope, Situation Overview, and Planning Assumptions. Includes general statements about the following subjects:

- What the EOP is designed to do.

- The scope of the emergency response as well as the juvenile justice residential facility and geographic area to which the plan applies.

- The geographic characteristics and hazards of the region in which the facility is located, data about the facility's physical plant and its staff and residents, and how the facility expects to receive or provide assistance within regional response structures.

- Basic emergency planning assumptions (e.g., the possibility of a heightened need for medical and mental/behavioral health services).

A sample format for the Purpose, Scope, Situation Overview, and Planning Assumptions section for a juvenile justice residential facility's EOP is shown on page 9.

Concept of Operations (CONOPS). Establishes in broad terms the sequence and scope of the planned emergency response. It is a written statement or visual representation showing generally how the EOP will be executed. Included in the CONOPS are the operational activities involved in—

- Identifying and assessing the hazard.

- Selecting protective action.

- Notifying families, staff, external partners, and the public.

- Addressing short- and long-term needs of staff and residents.

- Ensuring the continued operation of the physical plant.

Organization and Assignment of Responsibilities. Provides a list of the kinds of tasks to be performed (and the job titles of the individuals responsible for carrying out the tasks) without the procedural details included in the annexes. Both primary and supporting responsibilities should be assigned.

Direction, Control, and Coordination. Identifies who has tactical and operational control of the emergency response. Describes the facility's Incident Command System (ICS), a standardized, all-hazards management approach that helps to ensure a coordinated response. Also indicates how the ICS interfaces with other emergency command structures in the community or state if the facility's ICS is part of a larger response operation.

Information Collection, Analysis, and Dissemination. Describes the information that is essential to operations. Identifies the sources of the information, who is authorized to share the information, how and in what format the information is to be shared, and the circumstances that require the information.

Communications. Offers general information about protocols for communication between the juvenile

Sample Section of Emergency Operations Plan:
Purpose, Scope, Situation Overview, and Planning Assumptions

Purpose

The purpose of this plan is to ensure that [Name of Juvenile Justice Residential Facility]'s critical functions can continue to be carried out during an emergency and to define the actions and roles necessary for an effective and coordinated emergency response. The basic plan provides guidance before, during, and after an emergency. The plan takes a systematic approach to addressing all hazards through emergency management and planning for mitigation/prevention, preparedness, response, and recovery efforts.

Scope

This plan applies to [Name of Juvenile Justice Residential Facility/Juvenile Justice Agency] within the geographical boundary of [Name of City/County].

Situation Overview

Characteristics

[Name of Jurisdiction] includes [Name of Juvenile Justice Residential Facility] located at [Physical Address]. [Name of Juvenile Justice Residential Facility] consists of [number] main buildings, [number] portable structures/buildings, [number] living/programming buildings, [number] beds, [number] recreation fields, [number] other outdoor areas for programming, and [number] parking areas. In addition, the center includes the following buildings: [utility buildings, storage, etc.].

Demographics

[Name of Juvenile Justice Residential Facility] currently houses a total of [number] residents. The facility is currently meeting the access and functional needs of [number] residents with disabilities. Following is a breakdown of the number of employees:

> Security: [number].
> Medical, case management, and mental/behavioral health: [number].
> School: [number].
> Support (human resources, business office): [number].
> Janitorial/custodial/maintenance: [number].
> Food services: [number].
> Other (includes specialty and contract staff and volunteers): [number].

Hazard Profile

A vulnerability assessment completed on [date] has determined that [Name of Juvenile Justice Residential Facility] is at risk of experiencing disruptions in day-to-day operations as a result of the following emergencies: [wildfires, floods, hazardous material spills, hurricanes, earthquakes, tornadoes, extreme heat and cold, tsunamis, landslides, terrorist threats, civil unrest, nuclear accidents, aircraft accidents, war-related disasters, utility failures, hostage crises, sexual assaults, bomb threats, and public health and medical emergencies.]

Planning Assumptions

- In a major emergency, there will be a surge in the need for medical and mental/behavioral health services.
- Staff and residents will sustain injuries of varying degrees of severity.
- Security issues will arise.
- Support from outside the facility will be limited for the first 72 hours.
- Staff have been trained in emergency protocols and procedures.

NOTE: This sidebar was created with the assistance of Donald Lumpkins, Chief, Planning and Assistance Branch, National Preparedness Directorate, Federal Emergency Management Agency.

justice residential facility, response organizations, and other partners.

Administration, Finance, and Logistics. Outlines general support requirements and the availability of services and support for emergencies, as well as policies for administering resources. Includes requirements for tracking expenditures and the use of resources.

Plan Development and Maintenance. Discusses the overall approach to planning and the assignment of development and maintenance responsibilities. Identifies by position the individuals responsible for developing, revising, and approving the basic plan and annexes. Outlines a schedule for review of the EOP and directives for regular emergency-preparedness training for staff.

Authorities and References. Describes the legal basis for emergency operations and contains references to important documents on which the plan is based.

Annexes

Functional Annexes. Focus on specific policies, procedures, roles, responsibilities, and operational actions that agencies and departments carry out before, during, and after a range of emergencies. Also establish preparedness targets (training, exercises, equipment checks, etc.).

Hazard-Specific Annexes. Usually identify hazard-specific risk areas and evacuation routes, specify

provisions and protocols for warning the public and disseminating emergency public information, and specify the types of protective equipment and detection devices responders will use. Typically include maps, charts, tables, checklists, resource inventories, and summaries of critical information for each emergency the juvenile justice residential facility is at risk of experiencing.

Approving and Disseminating the Plan

The written plan should be checked to ensure conformity with applicable federal, state, county, and local standards and presented to the appropriate officials for signature. The juvenile justice residential facility's staff attorney, who should be engaged throughout every phase of the EOP's development, ensures that the EOP is aligned with statutes across all levels of government, protects the rights of staff and youth, and reduces potential liabilities for the juvenile justice agency and the juvenile justice residential facility. In addition, the following individuals should be included in the approval process:

- Director of the juvenile justice agency and/or director of the juvenile justice residential facility.

- Deputy/assistant director of the facility.

- Chief of security/safety officer.

- Medical director.

- Human resources director.

- Business manager.

- Activity director.

Human resources staff or trainers should ensure that each new employee at the facility is familiar with and has easy access to the plan. EOPs should be accessible online (and secured for staff only). In addition, a hardcopy version of the plan should be readily accessible in each of the facility's departments for reference purposes.

As a staff-development assignment, new employees might be required to identify which components of the plan pertain to their job responsibilities. Significant sections of the EOP could be highlighted as standing professional development curriculum topics for all existing staff. In addition, trainers could provide a quick review of a specific section of the plan or could prepare materials for the highest ranking staff member to share with others when leading roll call.

Dissemination of the plan extends to the larger community as well. Juvenile justice residential facilities should distribute the EOP to the appropriate emergency management agency and juvenile justice agency.

Exercising the Plan and Evaluating Its Effectiveness

There is no better way to determine whether an EOP is effective than to test it during drills and exercises. These exercises, which should be announced as well as unannounced, will enable the facility's leadership to quickly identify where gaps need to be filled in the plan and where employee skills require further development. Youth may also be included in drills, and their feedback should be included in the review and revision process.

During drills, it is recommended that observers be present to provide objective feedback on how the drill proceeded, whether the plan was followed and properly executed by staff, and whether the alert system and equipment functioned as expected. The purpose of the drill is to teach the plan, identify flaws in its content, and enhance emergency response by revising the plan. Formalized feedback from these drills is an essential foundation for the further refinement and improvement of the facility's emergency response capability. Feedback might be obtained through a form distributed to heads of major departments (e.g., security, medical services, education) by the juvenile justice residential facility's director or assistant director.

FEMA/Jocelyn Augustino

Following are some examples of questions that might be included on the feedback form:

- What components of the EOP worked well?

- Did these components impact, or were they impacted by, other sections of the EOP?

- What components did not work well?

- Did these components impact, or were they impacted by, other sections of the EOP?

- If the EOP did not work well in certain areas, what corrective actions are recommended?

- Which individuals (by job title) are authorized to alter emergency operations procedures?

Reviewing, Revising, and Maintaining the Plan

The EOP should be updated as new information becomes available and as gaps in existing procedures are identified. Assessments should focus on whether there is a need to—

- Clarify the plan's directives and procedures.

- Expand the support or resources required for the safety of youth and staff.

- Request the assistance of additional community
  stakeholders.

- Improve the effectiveness of the communications
  strategy and of transportation procedures.

- Obtain additional forms and documents.

- Facilitate access to resources.

- Adjust tools used for coordinated planning.

New community partnerships established during the
response and recovery phases of an emergency must
be sustained and incorporated into the EOP as it is
revised following an emergency. These stakeholders
should be involved in the revision process. The updated
EOP should be shared with partnering agencies (e.g.,
law enforcement, child welfare, education, labor, substance abuse, and mental health organizations) for their
information and coordinated response. Peer agencies
often face similar challenges and will benefit from sharing lessons learned during an emergency.

During the process of review and revision, youth's
families should be offered an opportunity to share
their perspectives on what worked and what did not.
The facility's lead officials may wish to hold town
hall-style meetings following an emergency. Families
can offer their insights, and the leadership can communicate lessons learned during the emergency. All
of these interchanges will help reinforce the facility's
partnership with the surrounding community and will
be an important step in enhancing the facility's EOP.

FEMA/Jocelyn Augustino

Section 2: Budgeting for Emergency Planning and Response

Adequate fiscal resources help ensure the effectiveness of a facility's preparation for, response to, and recovery from an emergency. Facilities should purposefully budget to cover the cost of drills as well as that of equipment, supplies, and compensation of staff for overtime work during an emergency.

The budget should also address long-term evacuation expenses in the event that the response and recovery phases are lengthy. Issues such as the cost of housing for staff and charges incurred as guests at a host facility should be included in the budget planning. Fiscal needs should be reported to the governmental entity that oversees the facility's management and budget.

The facility's policy for emergency planning should stipulate that allowances will be made for the reallocation of funds during an emergency. The emergency operations plan should clearly identify (by job title) the individuals in the juvenile justice agency and juvenile justice residential facility who have the authority to approve a reallocation of funds.

When a major emergency occurs, the leadership of the juvenile justice residential facility may consider outside sources of assistance. The facility and the

FEMA/Patsy Lynch

juvenile justice agency might partner with the state's emergency management agency and, in the event of a federally declared disaster, with the Federal Emergency Management Agency.

Finally, juvenile justice residential facilities should make certain that contracts exist and are current for supplies and services that will be needed before, during, and following an emergency. It may be necessary to arrange contracts with local vendors who have a large distribution network in the event that the local vendor's operation is disrupted by a long-term emergency.

Section 3: Allocating Responsibilities to Staff

The effectiveness of an emergency response depends to a great degree on ensuring that all staff are fully briefed on their roles. Responsibilities in the event of an emergency must be clearly assigned, both to staff and to other cooperating agencies and organizations. Coordination requirements with other agencies should also be described.[7] Those whose responsibilities might be specified include:

- The facility's director.

- Security personnel.

- Maintenance staff.

- Transportation providers.

- Law enforcement agencies.

- Firefighters.

- Emergency medical services personnel.

- Public works officials and/or agencies.

The Incident Command System (ICS), which specifies the organizational structure, decisionmaking authority, and procedures for managing emergencies, is the tool by which the facility will assign responsibilities to staff. It is the most effective method for ensuring successful continuity of operations in a facility when an emergency occurs.

The ICS should be directly tied to the state, county, and local emergency command systems. A member of the facility's staff may also be a member of the emergency command system in the surrounding community. He or she may be the ideal individual to

FEMA/Jocelyn Augustino

oversee coordination with outside agencies and to assist with revisions to the facility's emergency operations plan (EOP) in the weeks and months following an emergency. More information on creating an ICS is available at the Federal Emergency Management Agency's online ICS Resource Center, at training. fema.gov/FMIWeb/IS/ICSResource/index.htm

Juvenile justice residential facility administrators may consider appointing and training one incident commander and two or three staff members to serve as backup commanders. This measure will enable the facility to continue operations in the event that the designated commander is unexpectedly unable to report for duty. It also allows for a rotation system that ensures coverage 24 hours a day, 7 days a week. Incident commanders should be members of the team that writes, reviews, and assesses the facility's EOP. Throughout each phase of the preparedness cycle, the commanders should maintain regular communication with the facility's other lead official(s) to ensure that these authorities are kept up to date.

---

[7] For example, the decision to evacuate and the implementation of an evacuation plan may be the responsibility of firefighters. In this case, the fire department would function as the lead agency, with the juvenile justice residential facility assuming a secondary role.

Identifying Essential Staff and Clarifying Their Responsibilities

Staff members designated "essential" — staff whose responsibilities can only be carried out onsite (e.g., maintenance staff, dormitory supervisors, security personnel) — should have their roles and responsibilities specified in a written document. This document should be signed to ensure accountability. No staff positions are more critical than those involving the direct supervision and care of youth. The young people entrusted to the facility's care must have staff to oversee them and keep them safe and secure. Backup staff must be identified in the event that designated staff are unavailable during an emergency.

The delineation of roles and responsibilities should include a statement that evacuation may be necessary in an emergency and that certain staff will be required to work in alternate locations, which may necessitate separation from their families for an extended period. The statement should indicate that, in the event of an evacuation, staff must report for work (barring extraordinary circumstances, to be specified in the plan) or remain available on standby to relieve other staff. The statement should identify which staff will evacuate with youth and specify how long they will be expected to

remain on duty before they are relieved by other staff. The plan should designate staff members on the relief team and provide information about when and where they should report to relieve staff who have evacuated. Plans should call for at least two rotating teams during the evacuation.

To assist staff in understanding their specific roles and those of their colleagues in responding to and recovering from an emergency, it is recommended that simple, concise "job action sheets" be created for quick reference. The job action sheets should align closely with staff's individual skill areas and with the directives outlined in the EOP.

A sample job action sheet, currently used by the Rivarde Detention Center in Jefferson Parish, LA, is shown below. Job action sheets are particularly effective when they are formatted as checklists. For more information about job action sheets and for additional examples, see *A Guide for the Management of Emergencies or Other Unusual Incidents within Public Health Agencies* (Qureshi, Gebbie, and Gebbie, 2006), available at www.ualbanycphp.org/pinata/phics/guide/phics08.cfm.

Sample Evacuation Job Action Sheet

Position: Assistant Supervisor 1

Designation: Evacuation Coordinator

Duties:

- ☐ Ensure that all food, medical supplies, and clothing have been loaded in the evacuation vans.
- ☐ Ensure that all necessary medical and detention records of detainees to be evacuated are in the portable lock file and that the keys are given to escort supervisors.
- ☐ Ensure that communications equipment is loaded and that the communications protocol for evacuation is active.
- ☐ Ensure that parents of detainees to be evacuated have been informed of the evacuation site and given contact information.
- ☐ Ensure that there is an adequate supply of restraints.
- ☐ Ensure that all vehicles are in the staging area and are fully fueled and prepared.
- ☐ Contact the evacuation site and provide a timetable for movement.
- ☐ Coordinate with the Jefferson Parish Sheriff's Office for an evacuation escort.

Section 4: Establishing Communications Procedures

A juvenile justice residential facility's emergency operations plan (EOP) should outline clear procedures for internal and external communication. Special consideration should be given to communication with—

- Staff and their families.

- State, county, and local stakeholders.

- The general public.

- Youth's families.

Deciding in advance on methods for disseminating information can go a long way toward ensuring stability, order, and the effective implementation of the plan when an emergency occurs.

Internal Communication

If staffing needs can be predicted hours or days ahead of an impending emergency, staff can be kept informed about when they need to report for work or about other actions they may be required to take. During an emergency, it may be necessary to replace or supplement staff on account of illness, injury, exhaustion, or the need for additional manpower or expertise. After an emergency, the knowledge, commitment, and skills of staff will be necessary to facilitate a return to normal operations. For these reasons, contact information and an established protocol for communications with staff must be maintained.

A phone tree and a staff call-in system are effective methods for passing on vital information. The EOP would ideally designate one easily accessed call-in number for staff to use. Staff could call in at set times twice a day, at which time information and updates can be communicated. One advantage to this method is its efficiency: the facility's emergency operations

officials are not required to spend valuable time locating staff who are offsite. E-mail or text messages also might be used to contact staff.

FEMA/Jacinta Quesada

Do not count on a local line to be in service, as many emergencies will render local telephone systems unusable. A toll-free national phone line can establish a viable link to convey important information to staff and their families. In addition, a recording device on the line could allow staff to leave current contact information and messages about conditions in their area. Call lists could be organized by geographical area in the event that it becomes necessary to travel to employees' homes (or to a prearranged, easily accessible location in the community) to communicate in person when telephone or Internet communication fails.

Nonessential staff—employees whose duties can be performed offsite—do not need to put their safety in jeopardy by reporting to work during or following an emergency. Arrangements should be made for remote computer access or telework capabilities to ensure that these employees can continue to support operations. For example, a business manager could work remotely to ensure that payroll, supplies, and other necessities continue to be inventoried, ordered, and delivered in a timely manner.

Planners should also prepare for the possibility that the primary communication system—whether it be the telephone or the Internet—could fail during an emergency. At this point, other forms of communication (e.g., two-way radios and satellite phones) would need to be activated. Steps should be taken to ensure that an adequate supply of this equipment is on hand for continuity of operations. In some situations, particularly during an evacuation, support equipment such as car chargers, solar chargers, or hand-crank chargers would become necessary to keep communication devices operational.

External Communication

It is essential to develop procedures for communication with partnering agencies and organizations in the region, such as neighboring juvenile justice residential facilities, emergency management agencies, local law enforcement agencies, the courts, probation departments, medical services, and others.

As noted earlier, coordination should be an important part of the early planning stages. This coordination may take the form of memorandums of understanding, contracts, informal agreements, and interagency tabletop drills[8] that will help ensure that operations continue smoothly throughout the response and recovery phases. For legal, logistical, and numerous other reasons, a method of contacting and remaining in contact with other facilities and agencies in the region should be established.

Interagency communication during an emergency can be one of the most difficult things to establish. It is also one of the most critical. Advance agreements should specify which mode of communication will be used in the event of an emergency. Conference calls (at a specific time, or using a specifically set-aside emergency telephone number), established radio nets, a designated meeting place, a cell- or satellite-phone relay, or other methods can serve this purpose. The agreements should include backup plans.

In communications with the media and the general public, juvenile justice residential facilities should adhere to established policies. One spokesperson (e.g., the press secretary or lead administrator) should be designated to oversee the release of all information. This approach helps ensure clear communication and a consistent message. All releases should be prepared with guidance from the lead emergency staff member and/or appropriate professional (e.g., medical doctor, lead mental health clinician). The releases should be reviewed and approved by the appropriate leadership. Information disseminated to the public should be on a strictly need-to-know basis; only essential information is required. The names of youth (as well as other identifying information) should not be included.

Procedures should be in place for notifying families in a timely manner about the nature of the emergency and the facility's plans for ensuring the safety of youth. Families should also be kept well informed about the facility's procedures for releasing youth to their families in the event that an evacuation becomes necessary. At the onset of any threat, families should be

---

[8] Tabletop drills involve key personnel in discussions of simulated scenarios in an informal setting. These exercises can be used to assess plans, policies, and procedures to prevent, respond to, and recover from a specific emergency (Federal Emergency Management Agency, 2007b).

made aware of what steps will be taken to ensure the safety and security of youth in custody. If time allows in a major emergency requiring evacuation, families should be informed about whether their children are likely to be released or moved to another facility outside the immediate geographical area.

Staff should consult families regularly about their children's needs. Information supplied by families might include special instructions for youth with reading disabilities, dietary guidelines, and the need for medication or specialized equipment and training to address medical issues such as asthma and diabetes. This will be a helpful supplement to the information staff already have on hand from medical records, their own observations, and information provided by youth. In the event that youth can be released to their families during an evacuation, this ongoing contact enables staff to locate families and coordinate the release with families in a safe and efficient manner.

Each family should provide the following information with regular updates to the appropriate staff during visitation days and other contacts with the facility:

- Contact information at the location a family is most likely to travel to in the event that they must evacuate their homes.

- The phone numbers, names, and pertinent contact information for relatives who live in another region or out of state. This information will assist youth who qualify for release from the facility during an emergency but who cannot locate their own families.

- The cell phone numbers of at least two relatives who would know the family's whereabouts in an emergency.

Additional guidelines for keeping families regularly informed and assisting youth in contacting their families during an emergency are available in section 10, "Offering Support to Youth and Their Families."

Section 5: Planning To Protect Critical Infrastructure

A juvenile justice residential facility's critical infrastructure is defined as systems and assets—either physical or virtual—that are so vital that their incapacitation or destruction may have a debilitating effect on a facility's security, operations, and environment, and on the safety and well-being of youth and staff.[9]

Physical infrastructure includes:

- The physical plant.

- Communications technology (e.g., telephones, satellite phones, radios).

- Utilities (e.g., water, gas, electricity, sewage).

- Transportation vehicles (in case of evacuation or medical transfer).

- Hardcopy vital records.

Virtual infrastructure includes:

- Youth records maintained in an electronic database.

- Operations records maintained in an electronic database.

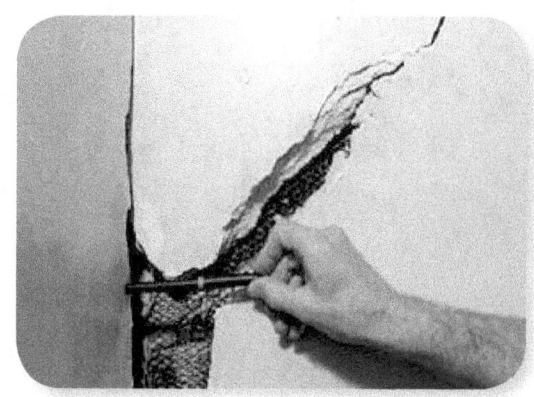

FEMA/Adam Dubrowa

- Information technology (e.g., servers, desktop computers, laptops, smartphones, and other communications devices).

Protecting critical infrastructure from exposure, damage, or destruction may involve incorporating hazard resistance into initial facility design, building in resiliency and redundancy, installing security systems, and implementing cyber-security measures.

---

[9] This text is adapted from the definition of critical infrastructure supplied in Section 1016(e) of Public Law 107–56 (42 U.S.C. 5195(e)), also known as The USA PATRIOT Act: "Systems and assets, whether physical or virtual, so vital to the United States that the incapacity or destruction of such systems and assets would have a debilitating impact on security, national economic security, national public health or safety, or any combination of these matters."

Critical Infrastructure Protection

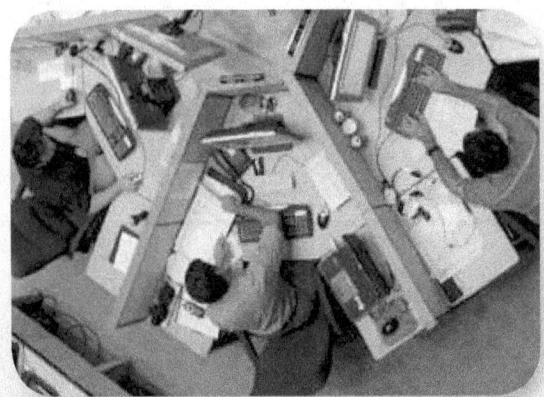

FEMA/Mark Wolfe

Emergency managers use a process known as Critical Infrastructure Protection, which consists of the following steps:

1. Identify critical infrastructure that must remain continuously intact and operational to ensure that a facility's essential functions can be carried out.

2. Determine the threat posed by all possible hazards to the critical infrastructure.

3. Analyze the vulnerabilities or weaknesses that exist in the infrastructure.

4. Assess the risk of the degradation or loss of the threatened/ vulnerable infrastructure.

5. Apply protective or resiliency measures to reduce risk, protect infrastructure, or ensure the rapid restoration of infrastructure after an emergency.

Section 6: Preparing To Shelter in Place and To Evacuate

Sheltering in place typically involves retaining staff and youth in a predetermined area for a short period of time to avoid danger or prevent harm. Under these circumstances, regular activities such as school and recreation are suspended, and the focus shifts to ensuring safety and maintaining security. Situations that require sheltering in place may include tornadoes, chemical spills, street flooding, civil unrest, and terrorist incidents. Each of these emergencies requires special precautions.

For example, tornadoes can appear without warning, so preparations and decisions about how and where to shelter must be made well in advance. Staff must immediately direct youth and other employees to a designated area away from windows or exterior doors. The ideal locations are interior rooms (or hallways) on the lowest possible floor. Youth and staff should sit in close proximity in a curled position with arms over their heads for protection and remain quiet until an all-clear signal is given.

During a chemical spill, the facility's officials will need to plan for closing all doors and windows and turning off all furnaces, air conditioners, or other ventilation equipment. It may also be necessary to place plastic sheeting over windows and vents and to place duct tape over electrical outlets, around doors, and over other openings.

Evacuation requires more indepth planning. Arrangements need to be made to move to an alternate facility, to develop protocols for effective transportation, to maintain security, and to ensure the well-being of staff and residents as they adjust to a major disruption to their normal day-to-day activities. Situations that may require evacuation to an alternate location may include hurricanes, flooding in the facility caused by rising water, wildfires, volcanic eruptions, long-term hazardous materials or radiological releases, and other natural and manmade emergencies.

During an evacuation, staff will need to quickly and efficiently move youth, other employees, equipment (e.g., communications and medical equipment), supplies (e.g., bedding and clothing), food, and appropriate records to an alternate location until the conditions that caused the evacuation have abated and it has been determined that it is safe for youth and staff to return. Planners should ensure that all vehicles (including escort vehicles) have two-way radio communication capabilities and that an appropriate number of restraints (plastic flex cuffs) are available.

A vulnerability assessment conducted during the planning phase will have identified the emergencies likely to occur in a specific geographical area, and this will assist the facility in preparing for those emergencies and determining ahead of time which types of events would most likely require sheltering in place and which types would require evacuation.

As with all aspects of emergency preparedness, there should be plans for backup in case emergency procedures fail or staff are unable to report for duty. At least one alternate method or person should always be available.

Ensuring the Availability of Adequate Supplies

During the planning phase, separate supply lists should be created for sheltering in place and for evacuating from a facility. The supplies required to carry out each of these procedures are quite distinct.

Creating separate lists will prevent unnecessary confusion and major delays during an emergency. The lists should be easily accessible to ensure a quick emergency response.

FEMA/Michael Rieger

Planners should be certain that there are enough supplies to shelter in place for at least 72 hours as it may not be possible to replenish supplies after an emergency strikes. Planners should anticipate that for several days supply lines may be severed, and the following essential supplies should be stored accordingly:

• Food and drinking water.

• First-aid supplies.

• Generators.

• Space heaters.

• Chemical toilets.

• Flashlights.

• Batteries.

Although most evacuations are to a designated facility that has agreed to provide most essential provisions, contingency plans should be made to bring enough

supplies for 3–5 days. These supplies, included in what is commonly known as a "drive-away kit," may not need to be used; however, if a shortage develops, the supplies could become critical. This measure will also ensure an adequate supply of essential items if the primary evacuation site cannot be reached in a timely fashion or is not immediately available. These items should include:

• Food and drinking water.[10]

• First-aid supplies.

• Portable medical records.

• Medication.

• Portable emergency generators.

• Clothing.

• Hygiene supplies.

• Bedding and tents.

• Communications equipment (e.g., cell phones and radios).

• Flashlights.

• Batteries.

• Charged laptops.

• Additional fuel for vehicles.

Selecting Evacuation Sites

During the planning phase, agreements should be signed with a receiving facility and one or more backup facilities that have the capacity to support staff and residents. It is important to choose at least one location that is far enough away that it is unlikely to be

---

[10] Juvenile justice residential facilities may wish to consider limiting the amount of perishable food and focus instead on bringing canned, vacuum-sealed, dry, and powdered foods. Another option would be to sign a contract for food and water services with a vendor in the community to which the facility will be evacuating as a backup measure in the event that the food services operation at the host facility is unable to meet the demand. The provision of food services should be spelled out in the agreement between the host center and the evacuating facility.

affected by an emergency in the facility's geographical area. Agreements should establish the criteria, requirements, and needs of the evacuating facility. It is important to specify what sections of the receiving facility the evacuated youth and staff will occupy and what essentials the receiving facility will provide. These essentials would typically include the following items:

- Food, water, and bedding.

- Separate areas for staff to rest, shower, and sleep.

- The use of computer equipment and the Internet.

It is critical that both the staff of the juvenile justice residential facility and the staff of the host facility be fully briefed on their respective responsibilities. Agreements should be reviewed and renewed annually.

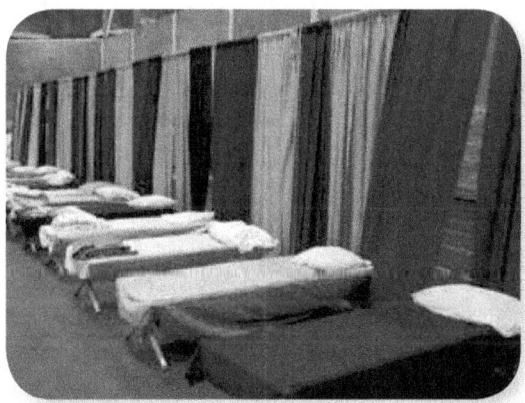

FEMA/Liz Roll

Juvenile justice planners should be certain that any site housing a detained juvenile population complies with the core protections of the Juvenile Justice and Delinquency Prevention (JJDP) Act of 1974, as amended.[11] State, county, or local juvenile detention facilities may be an ideal choice as these facilities are regularly monitored for compliance with the JJDP Act. In addition, these facilities should already comply with other guidelines promoted by professional correctional organizations and agency policies. A visit to a potential evacuation site during the planning phase could be a helpful way to eliminate any questions that may exist about compliance with the JJDP Act. Under no circumstances should juvenile justice residential facilities plan to evacuate to facilities that hold adults if those facilities do not provide adequate sight-and-sound separation of juveniles from the adult population.

Preparations for evacuating youth or receiving youth from another facility should take into account gender and safety issues. There should be separate areas for each gender. Staffing considerations should include appropriate coverage by direct-care staff of the same gender.

Finally, the facility's staff will need to plan strategically to address issues associated with high-risk populations (e.g., serious mental health disorders, violent behavior, a history of escape). Planning ahead for disciplinary issues during an evacuation will help promote the safety of staff and of other youth in the facility.

Developing Protocols for the Release of Youth to Their Families

An agreement with the local juvenile court should be made well in advance to identify procedures for releasing some of the youth to their families in the event that an evacuation is necessary. The juvenile justice residential facility and the court could determine which youth can be released to families and which should remain in custody. Procedures for the release of youth could include facility and court teleconferencing or signing orders via e-mail if inperson communication is impossible. Youth who remain in custody should be evacuated.

---

[11] The original goals of the JJDP Act were to help state and local governments prevent and control juvenile delinquency and to improve the juvenile justice system. These goals were reaffirmed in the reauthorization of the Act in 2002. Through the 2002 JJDP Act reauthorization, the Act's four core protections were maintained. Participating states must comply with these core protections to receive full funding under the Formula Grants program. They require the following: deinstitutionalization of status offenders, separation of juveniles from adults in secure facilities, removal of juveniles from adult jails and lockups, and reducing disproportionate minority contact within the juvenile justice system. For more information about the JJDP Act, visit OJJDP's Web site at ojjdp.gov/about/legislation.html.

If there is adequate time before an emergency strikes, families should be informed about whether the youth is likely to be released or evacuated. If the facility waits too long to make a decision, families may evacuate their own homes before they can be contacted to secure their child.

Families of youth who can be released should be contacted as soon as possible and instructed to retrieve their children from the facility. However, families may not be able to travel to the facility in a major emergency that affects the larger community; ideally, emergency planning should establish procedures for the facility to transport youth to their families.

Addressing Transportation Issues

The facility's buses will transport youth who must remain in secure care to the host facility. When possible, all supplies, medical and mental health records, and other necessities should be loaded as soon as a threat requiring evacuation has been detected. The emergency operations plan should identify a staging area where vehicles can be loaded and prepared for immediate evacuation. After the vehicles are loaded with youth and staff, the staging area is the recommended location for any escort vehicles (e.g., police cars) to meet in preparation for the evacuation.

Evacuation routes should be established in advance. Alternate routes should be identified in anticipation of the possibility that the primary route cannot be used. Detailed maps and text directions should also be available, and copies should be stored in a central location to facilitate distribution at the time of evacuation.

During the planning phase, juvenile justice residential facilities should develop agreements with the appropriate law enforcement agency to provide escorts and priority access to alternate routes in case the primary routes are blocked. Without this advance preparation, youth and staff may find themselves in traffic for many hours during a major emergency, a frustrating situation that could lead to disciplinary problems and threats to the security and safety of evacuees.

FEMA/Patsy Lynch

If it is anticipated that additional vehicles or fuel may be needed from another source during an evacuation, facility officials should outline clearly in the planning phase when and how they are to be procured. Gas tanks should be full at all times as fuel may become scarce or completely unavailable during an emergency. At the first sign of an impending emergency, any vehicle that could possibly be used for evacuation should be filled with gas if it has been used for a purpose other than evacuation.

The state juvenile justice disaster plan should address preparations for youth leaving and entering the state, as these youth may now fall under the host facility's jurisdiction. A potentially helpful resource is the Interstate Compact for Juveniles (ICJ), which was created to regulate the interstate movement and supervision of juveniles, to ensure the public's safety, and to create a more effective and efficient means of transferring and tracking juveniles between states. Plans for evacuation should be developed on a regional basis in case it becomes necessary to evacuate youth across state lines. Regional planning also helps ensure that evacuated youth can remain as close to their homes and families as possible. The ICJ's governing body is the Interstate Commission for Juveniles. For more information on the ICJ, go to the Commission's Web site at www.juvenilecompact.org/.

If possible, staff should be dispatched in advance of the evacuation to assist in preparing the receiving facility for the evacuees' arrival. Although in many cases

FEMA/Michael Rieger

this may not be possible, it is an ideal way to ensure a smooth transition. The advance team may bring some supplies with them to further facilitate this movement. This team should include staff with sufficient authority to request changes in the original agreement with the host facility, if necessary.

Supporting Staff After an Evacuation

After the evacuation has been successfully carried out and residents and staff have been installed at the host facility, support services for staff should be made available. Particular attention should be paid to their medical and mental health needs. Staff will need to be given an opportunity to decompress and talk with professionals about their experiences.

For evacuated staff who are working at a host facility that is far from their homes, staff quarters could be established at the facility or in rooms rented outside the facility. A daily home-cooked meal might be prepared for staff. It may be helpful to arrange for staff to eat together as a team so they can exchange information about their homes and loved ones. Staff should be encouraged to speak with social services personnel and faith-based counselors as their concerns may increase significantly when they are separated from their families. As staff begin running out of their personal medication, the agency should arrange to have their medication refilled and also assist with payment, as many staff may not have access to funds. In addition, staff may need access to the Internet to contact vendors to obtain supplies, conduct personal business (e.g., assistance from the Federal Emergency Management Agency, food stamps, bill payments), and communicate with their relatives.

Section 7: Providing Mental Health Services and Medical Care

When a major emergency arises, there may be a surge in the need for services to address the mental health and medical needs of youth and staff. It is important to plan ahead for a range of emergencies. During a major emergency, for example, a well-planned triage procedure will help ensure that those who are most severely impacted either emotionally or physically by the event are treated as soon as possible.

Planning Ahead

During the planning phase, it is critical for juvenile justice residential facilities to establish "as-needed" contracts with mental and behavioral health professionals so they can assist in the event that onsite professionals are not available, or in the event that additional personnel above and beyond the facility's staff are needed. During the writing of the juvenile justice residential facility's emergency operations plan (EOP), these professionals should develop protocols for screening and assessment. A supply of these protocols should be available in multiple locations to ensure easy access.

The protocols should clearly outline the necessary steps personnel should take to address the mental and behavioral health needs of the most severely impacted youth following the emergency, as well as

plans for providing Psychological First Aid,[12] bereavement support, and other brief supportive services to all residents. Plans should be in place to address these needs in a continuum-of-care or four-tiered model that includes brief supportive services, individual treatment by a qualified mental or behavioral health professional at the juvenile justice residential facility, placement in a specialized mental health unit at the facility, and placement in an offsite mental health facility.

To ensure that the medical needs of physically injured staff and youth are met, agreements between a juvenile justice residential facility and a hospital in the immediate area typically are signed during the planning phase. This measure will prove to be extremely helpful in the event that some of the injuries sustained during an emergency exceed the healthcare capabilities of onsite medical personnel. It is recommended that an agreement be signed with a secondary hospital in the

FEMA/Robert Kaufmann

---

[12] Psychological First Aid (PFA) is a supportive behavioral intervention for use in the immediate aftermath of disasters and other traumatic events. It does not assume that all youth will develop severe mental health problems or long-term difficulties, but instead is based on the understanding that youth in emergencies will experience a range of early physical, psychological, behavioral, and spiritual reactions that may be helped by support from compassionate and caring responders. PFA is designed to enhance safety; provide physical and emotional comfort; identify immediate needs and concerns; help establish contact with primary support persons or other sources of support, including family members, friends, and community resources; and provide information about stress reactions and coping. For more information, read the National Child Traumatic Stress Network's and the National Center for PTSD's *Psychological First Aid: Field Operations Guide, 2d Edition* (2008), at www.nctsnet.org/sites/default/files/pfa/english/1-psyfirstaid_final_complete_manual.pdf.

region in the event that the primary hospital is incapacitated by the emergency.

The EOP should address the possible need to waive established transportation procedures (e.g., placing youth in shackles and handcuffs) in order to transport seriously injured youth to a medical facility in the community as quickly as possible. In emergencies, security concerns should be weighed against the need to treat a serious medical problem.

In addition to addressing medical needs directly related to the emergency, the plan should outline procedures for continuing to treat preexisting or chronic medical conditions among youth and staff (e.g., diabetes, asthma, high blood pressure). Issues such as medication, treatment, the availability of medical supplies, and the maintenance of medical equipment must be addressed in the emergency plan.

Using a Triage System

During the response phase of a major emergency, mental health professionals, emergency medical services personnel, and facility staff who have the relevant qualifications should be assigned to determine who needs emergency first aid; secondary triage should be conducted to identify risk factors and symptoms of emotional distress or adjustment difficulties. If possible, one or two triage locations should be established where healthcare staff can assemble. A protocol for reporting to the triage location, developed by the juvenile justice residential facility's medical personnel, should be included in the EOP. The protocol should be practiced during drills.

Every effort should be made to use the facility's infirmary/sick-call area to treat youth and staff who are injured. If residents and staff have been evacuated, or if the infirmary is inaccessible or rendered inoperable by the emergency, it is recommended that a location be designated that is self-contained, has a noncontaminated water source, has electricity (it may be necessary to use a generator), and is easily accessible by medical emergency vehicles.

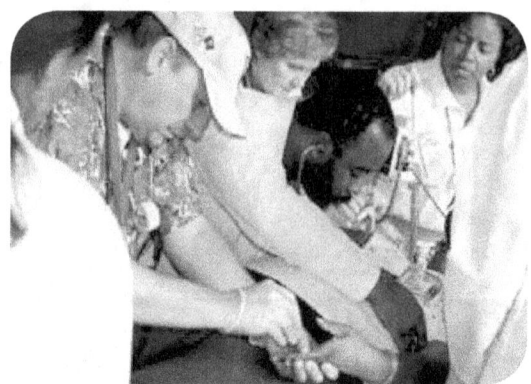

FEMA/George Armstrong

How One Juvenile Justice Residential Facility Conducted Triage

During a recent emergency, detained youth were evacuated to a secure-care facility operated by the state. A triage area was established in the facility's infirmary. Physicians (including psychiatrists), psychologists, nurses, and social workers were assigned to the triage area. Youth were hydrated immediately upon entry to the building and were quickly screened by the nurses and social workers. Each youth was then seen and assessed individually by the medical doctor and child psychiatrist as prioritized by nurses and social workers. A decision was made in each case about whether youth would remain in the infirmary for immediate treatment, would require hospitalization, or would be transferred to a different location on the site of the juvenile justice residential facility.

Youth who exhibit significant symptoms of distress during and following the emergency, or who are high risk on account of preexisting mental or behavioral health problems, should be further evaluated for suicidal ideation, psychosis, depression, and other issues identified by facility staff. The EOP should include immediate intervention strategies for emerging mental health issues.

Continuing Mental and Behavioral Health Assessments

Youth should be evaluated and monitored on an ongoing basis to determine the severity of their needs, especially during the early days of the recovery effort.

Youth usually respond appropriately during an emergency (e.g., following directions of direct-care personnel and other adults). However, youth with a history of mental or behavioral health issues, trauma, or loss may decompensate quickly after a major emergency, when the staff's attention is typically focused on getting the physical plant operational, restoring power, securing food, and dealing with other concerns. Facilities should ensure that these issues are addressed by qualified staff.

If youth develop serious mental health problems, professionals will recommend placement outside the juvenile justice residential facility. If transport is not possible during an emergency, staff should consider keeping youth who pose a danger to themselves or others in the infirmary and placing them under continuous observation until their condition improves or until they can be moved to a facility better equipped to address their needs.

If additional assistance is needed, facility officials may wish to consider temporarily relocating mental and behavioral health professionals from other facilities that were not impacted by the emergency or from community agencies with whom a memorandum of understanding has been signed to meet youth's immediate needs.

It is important to remember that staff, too, may be emotionally affected by an emergency. Staff who work directly with residents are critical to the well-being of these youth and can have a profound effect on their behavior. Many staff who are exhausted and experiencing stress while on duty may only require a brief, supportive conversation with nonsupervisory professionals in order to continue carrying out their assigned tasks effectively.

Volunteers on the facility's approved volunteer list (including individuals from the faith-based community) as well as nursing and mental and behavioral health staff should speak individually with the facility's employees on an ongoing basis to screen for stress-related

concerns, to informally assess their situation, and to offer support. Staff from the juvenile justice agency might be assigned to visit with employees to listen to their observations and recommendations about the facility's needs and about what measures may be taken to facilitate the performance of their duties.

Following an emergency, employees should be given permission to request a consultation with the facility's mental and behavioral health staff through a prescribed procedure (e.g., an employee assistance program). Referrals for additional treatment may be made to professionals in the community. Assessment of staff's needs should continue throughout the recovery phase.

FEMA/John Ficara

Integrating Emergency-Related Interventions Into Programming for Youth

Even youth who do not exhibit symptoms of serious mental health problems can benefit from continued support throughout the recovery phase after a major emergency. Staff may wish to consider integrating disaster-related interventions and brief supportive services into regular programming for youth, such as educational programming or substance abuse treatment. Weaving these interventions through the facility's routine daily activities can help continue to foster long-term adaptive functioning and coping skills.

Addressing Pandemics

The Federal Emergency Management Agency (FEMA) defines a pandemic as a global outbreak of disease that appears or "emerges" in the human population, spreading from person to person worldwide and causing serious illness.* Juvenile justice residential facilities and other congregate-care settings are especially vulnerable to the transmission of infectious disease.

Staff and youth should be educated about easy, common-sense measures they can take to protect themselves against infection. In addition, the facility's emergency operations plan (EOP) will most likely need to allow for the adjustment of intake and discharge procedures during a pandemic. The EOP might include a contingency plan to admit only juveniles who present the greatest danger to the community or who are at highest risk of escaping from the jurisdiction of the local detention center during the pandemic. Another measure might be to accept no admissions during the disease outbreak. The EOP should also include procedures for handling the health emergency should it escalate to the point that it is no longer safe for all youth to remain at the facility.

To minimize the spread of the disease, facilities will need to identify areas where youth exhibiting symptoms of disease may be quarantined and observed. Since FEMA guidelines indicate that at the height of a serious pandemic as much as 40 percent of the staff may be absent for up to 2 weeks, facilities should provide influenza vaccinations for all facility employees and identify potential replacements for staff. Staff replacements will need to be trained.

For comprehensive information about addressing pandemics, visit flu.gov, a federal Web site managed by the U.S. Department of Health and Human Services.

*Continuity of Operations: An Overview of Continuity Planning for Pandemic Influenza (Federal Emergency Management Agency, n.d.).

Section 8: Training Staff in Basic Emergency Care

Healthcare resources, both in the juvenile justice residential facility and in the community at large, may not be readily available in a major emergency. Training for frontline staff—particularly in first aid, cardiopulmonary resuscitation, and brief supportive interventions to address emotional trauma—is crucial to ensuring youth's safety and well-being. This training should be updated regularly and incorporated into regular drills.

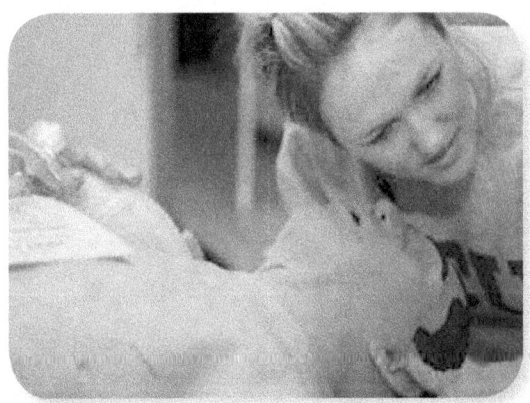

FEMA/Shannon Arledge

Many facilities have limited access to professional pediatric mental health providers on a day-to-day basis. In an emergency situation, access to mental health providers could be absent altogether. Staff should be trained to serve as a first line of defense against undiagnosed mental and behavioral health problems; they should be trained to recognize serious mental and behavioral health concerns and to bring them to the attention of the appropriate medical professionals.

A necessary component of this training model, especially for staff who have direct contact with youth, should focus on signs of distress and adjustment difficulties in youth during or following a catastrophic event. Training should include basic issues of mental health, characteristics typical of the juvenile justice population (including previous exposure to violence and a high incidence of mental health problems), how to identify symptoms of psychological trauma, the impact of bereavement and loss, and the nature of trauma-inducing events.

Training for staff and crisis counseling services for both youth and staff may be available through the Substance Abuse and Mental Health Services Administration's (SAMHSA's) Crisis Counseling Assistance and Training Program[13] or other state or federal programs. Such training can also be obtained through community and government mental health agencies or other partners. Juvenile justice residential facilities should coordinate with the state mental health agency before and after an emergency to determine what state and federal resources may be available. In addition, facilities might consider incorporating into their mandatory training instruction on identifying signs of distress in youth.

Immediately following a major emergency, refresher training should be held for staff who work in the residential facility's dormitories or school. During the weeks that followed a recent emergency, contracted mental health and medical professionals provided quick review sessions during shift roll call for frontline staff on the warning signs of psychological problems.

---

[13] To learn more about SAMHSA's Crisis Counseling Assistance and Training Program, go to store.samhsa.gov/product/SMA09-4373.

Section 9: Evaluating the Facility's Staffing Needs

Staff vacancies should be filled efficiently and quickly to minimize burnout, which can lead to the loss of additional employees. Because of accumulated fatigue, staff will likely become physically and mentally exhausted more quickly during the recovery phase as opposed to the response phase. Staff will require time away from the job to manage their own affairs if they and their families have been seriously impacted by the emergency.

In order to quickly fill staffing vacancies, special arrangements might be made to accelerate the hiring timeline. The facility's lead official could request special permission to suspend policies requiring a minimum score on a preemployment exam for entry-level work and instead hire staff who score within an acceptable range of the minimum. However, requirements for safety or background checks should not be waived under any circumstances.

The processes already in place to evaluate staffing needs should continue throughout the response and

FEMA/Andrea Booher

recovery phases, but more frequent assessments are recommended. The information gathered should be discussed with supervisory floor staff and administrators. An effective way to communicate staffing needs might be to incorporate administrators into roll call on a daily basis, especially in the initial days of the recovery phase. The evaluation of staffing needs should be a standing item on the agenda for staff meetings.

Section 10: Offering Support to Youth and Their Families

As facilities develop their emergency operations plans, considerable thought should be given to addressing the needs of youth and their families. Particularly during major and long-term emergencies, youth and their families will have a heightened need for programming, services, and support to regain a sense of stability and normalcy. In some cases, families may need to evacuate their homes and perhaps even the regions in which they live; these families will urgently need to relay information to their children about their location. Following are some examples of emergency planning that will help alleviate the anxiety of youth and their loved ones during an emergency.

Keeping Families Informed

Shortly after initial intake to the juvenile justice residential facility and the first contact with families, staff should provide information about how emergencies are handled. It is critical that families be made aware of the steps the facility will take (e.g., fire drills, shelter-in-place drills) to prepare for an emergency. Creating emergency information packets or a video/DVD with this information might be an efficient way to provide families with an overview of procedures for handling emergencies.

Families can be sources of valuable information as well. A survey or focus group could be organized on family visitation days to solicit emergency contact information and families' recommendations for the most effective methods for communicating with families, for ensuring regular contact with their children, and for continuing structured youth activities following an emergency until regular programming can be resumed.

Helping Youth To Contact Their Families

Youth in residential placement often experience an intense need for communication with family and loved ones during a crisis. Ordinarily, juvenile justice residential facilities have strict rules limiting the number of phone calls youth are allowed per week. Once the situation is stabilized, these rules should be relaxed to allow youth to contact their families more frequently. Staff can assist by setting reasonable limits on the number of calls. This communication serves as assurance for the family that their child is in a safe and secure location; it also keeps youth up to date on their families' status.

Shutterstock® Images

If the facility has designated hours on specific days of the week for family visits, it may pose a hardship on families affected by a major emergency. Facility staff should consider a more flexible visiting schedule, to the extent that staffing will allow. Given the difficulty of contacting family during major emergencies and the importance of such contacts for youth and their families, it is essential that ordinary rules limiting visits be suspended (within reason). The benefits of this may be more important than other services typically scheduled for that time period. During and following a disaster, youth and family stress can be reduced when family members have the opportunity to see each other and be assured that they are safe.

After an event, youth may be unable to reach family members at their normal phone numbers, especially during emergencies that necessitate a mass evacuation. Facilities should have procedures in place (possibly a toll-free national line) to enable families to contact the facility to report on their status and provide updated contact information. However, if the family has not been in touch with the facility or youth throughout the event, facilities should assist youth in reestablishing contact with their families. For more information, see the sidebar entitled "Resources for Family Reunification."

Providing Structured Activities for Youth

As staff and residents make the transition from the emergency response phase to recovery, the facility's lead officials should allow for flexibility in service organization and delivery. Staff shortages and other problems, such as physical plant malfunctions and power outages, will most likely require adjustments to regular activities. However, each day should approximate as much as possible the typical day a youth experienced before the emergency.

Resources for Family Reunification

Facilities should be familiar with established tools that can help assist with family reunification. In a federally declared disaster, the Federal Emergency Management Agency may activate the National Emergency Family Registry and Locator System and the National Emergency Child Locator Center to allow people who have been displaced and separated from their families to register and provide information about themselves and where they can be found (fema.gov). The American Red Cross operates Safe and Well (safeandwell. communityos.org/cms), which allows people displaced by a disaster to self-register and provide current contact information. In addition, Google may activate its similar system, Person Finder (google.com/crisisresponse/resources.html).

FEMA/Bob McMillan

After an emergency, lead officials and department heads should assess staffing needs, establish appropriate locations for programs and services, and create and disseminate a schedule of daily activities. These schedules should be posted in strategic locations around the facility. It is important to consider the unique needs of evacuated youth; they will need to reenroll in school, participate in recreational activities, receive support from volunteers, and be visited by their families. As soon as possible, contact with families, probation officers, and juvenile court officials; substance abuse treatment; and spiritual care should be resumed.

Although detained youth may require substantial support to help them recover from a major emergency, youth can also be part of the solution: they can use their skills in helping to rebuild the facility and assisting with cleanup and rebuilding efforts in the community to the extent that doing so is safe and practical. During formal group sessions or informal check-ins or conversations in the dormitory, staff can gather input from youth about which activities and functions they feel need to be put in place quickly. Youth might help make improvements to their surroundings (e.g., painting, decorating, rearranging furniture, cleaning). Those who are enrolled in vocational programming or who hold a vocational certificate could use their acquired skills to improve the quality of life for themselves and their peers.

Section 11: Meeting the Needs of Staff and Their Families

Emergencies can be particularly challenging for staff as they attempt to balance their obligations to their families with those to the facility and its residents. Because many staff are assigned to critical roles that involve the direct supervision of youth, plans must be made well ahead of time to ensure that staff's families are safe and that staff continue to be paid during an emergency. The personal needs of staff must be carefully considered in order to ensure that they are able to carry out their duties at the facility.

Encouraging Staff To Create Family Emergency Plans

Staff should be encouraged to establish plans (including backup plans) for their families, review the plans annually, and make necessary adjustments to the plans as circumstances change. Planning ahead in this way will help staff to remain calm in the event that an emergency affects their family while they are on call at the facility. It will also enable staff to carry out their professional responsibilities during an emergency. An employee who has not planned for the safety or evacuation of his family may not be able to report for work during an essential time. Information about creating a family emergency plan is available on the Federal Emergency Management Agency's (FEMA's) Web site, at fema.gov/plan/prepare/plan.shtm.

Ensuring That Staff Continue To Be Paid

During an emergency, payment of staff is often initially overlooked because of other critical needs. However, plans for continued payment must be made ahead of time so that staff and their families can meet their basic needs and remain financially secure. In major emergencies, staff may need to use their pay to subsidize their families' stay at a hotel or other costly

FEMA/Jerry DeFelice

venues, and payment must be available to cover these expenditures.

Payroll offices are increasingly requiring the use of direct deposits. This system is very practical during an evacuation, as it will eliminate the need to send staff to a designated area to retrieve paychecks and then find a place to cash them. This may not even be possible if local banks are affected by the emergency and are closed as a result. Whatever option is used, methods must be established to ensure that payment of staff continues throughout the emergency.

Allowing Staff To Exercise Control

During the response phase of an emergency, staff often face the challenge of making critical decisions as circumstances evolve minute by minute. Although the importance of following the written plan for the emergency response must be emphasized, employees should be granted the flexibility to use their own judgment in making decisions that are in the best interest of the residents, the staff, and the facility as a whole. If all decisions must be channeled through an approval process, there will be delays in critical action steps and missed opportunities to effectively address the emergency. Many of these staff-directed decisions can be reviewed in a daily debriefing and in ongoing training throughout the year.

Staff should also be encouraged to adjust their work schedules and the dress code to accommodate the requirements of an emergency. Staff might be allowed to use flex-time in order to not only meet the special emergency needs of the juvenile justice residential facility, but also to address their own personal or family concerns. In addition, if staff have offices in a section of the facility that has been damaged, staff should be consulted about their preferences regarding an alternate work location.

Arranging for Housing

Although the recovery phase for many emergencies is brief and alternate housing for staff often is not required, in major emergencies staff may have significant short- or long-term housing needs as a result of homes being damaged or destroyed. Staff may need assistance in locating suitable housing that meets the needs of their families and allows them to remain in proximity to the facility so they can continue performing their regular job duties. This may pose a significant challenge if facilities are forced to relocate to a remote location for an extended period following an emergency. Facilities can assist staff by helping to find suitable housing stock in the area. In addition, FEMA, state agencies, and/or case management programs may be able to provide assistance to staff to help locate suitable housing options.

Section 12: Managing Volunteers

Volunteers can be a tremendous asset to a juvenile justice residential facility following an emergency. All potential volunteers should be screened and approved according to the facility's requirements, especially volunteers who may have direct contact with youth. They should receive heightened scrutiny to ensure that they have the best interests of the youth in mind. The facility's approved volunteers can play a valuable role as mentors and as a source of emotional support to youth. Volunteers who have not yet been screened can assist with other critical tasks, including providing food, clothing, personal items, and other necessities.

FEMA/Dave Saville

During the planning phase, facility staff may want to identify community and faith-based organizations as resources for volunteers who can be activated in times of emergency. Outreach activities to encourage volunteer services should be conducted well in advance of an emergency; this will help ensure the appropriate screening of volunteers and the provision of high-quality services.

Conclusion

Effective emergency management requires collaboration at all levels—from the facility's senior officials, to department heads, to the staff who work in the dormitories, recreation areas, classrooms, and medical units. Commitment from the facility's leadership is especially important to establishing emergency planning as a top priority in the facility and integrating the planning with the facility's policies and procedures. Collaboration must also extend outward from the facility to a range of stakeholders in the surrounding community and region.

Juvenile justice residential facilities may find that the organizational tasks involved in comprehensively preparing for emergencies have the added benefit of improving day-to-day operations. The close coordination that is intrinsic to emergency planning can have a ripple effect as operations become more efficient and as risk to the facility's physical plant is reduced through appropriate prevention/mitigation measures.

Emergency preparedness is a continuous and, at times, complex process. The challenges may seem daunting. However, careful planning is critical to protecting youth and staff from injury and trauma, to continuing essential functions at juvenile justice residential facilities, and to minimizing disruptions to daily activities in the event of an emergency. Comprehensive preparedness for a range of emergencies is not an option, but a fundamental responsibility.

References and Resources

American Academy of Pediatrics. 2011. Promoting Adjustment and Helping Children Cope. Elk Grove Village, IL: American Academy of Pediatrics. Retrieved April 20, 2011, from the Web: aap.org/disasters/adjustment.cfm.

American Red Cross. 2011. Safe and Well. Washington, DC: American Red Cross. Retrieved April 22, 2011, from the Web: safeandwell.communityos.org/cms.

Andrews, S.J., and Yeres, S. 2006. *An Assessment of the Impact of Hurricanes Katrina and Rita on the Juvenile Justice System.* Retrieved April 4, 2011, from the Web: www.ncjrs.gov/App/publications/abstract.aspx?ID=256182.

Berne, R. 2009. *Disaster Preparedness Resource Guide for Child Welfare Agencies.* Baltimore, MD: The Annie E. Casey Foundation. Retrieved May 10, 2011, from the Web: www.aecf.org/~/media/Pubs/Topics/Child%20Welfare%20Permanence/Other/DisasterPreparednessResourceGuidefor ChildWelf/DisasterPrep.pdf.

Center for Network Development. Juvenile Information Sharing. Denver, CO: Center for Network Development. Retrieved April 22, 2011, from the Web: juvenileis.org.

Federal Emergency Management Agency. n.d. *Continuity of Operations: An Overview of Continuity Planning for Pandemic Influenza.* Washington, DC: U.S. Department of Homeland Security. Retrieved April 20, 2011, from the Web: fema.gov/pdf/about/org/ncp/pan_brochure.pdf.

Federal Emergency Management Agency. n.d. *Continuity of Operations Plan Template for Federal Departments and Agencies.* Washington, DC: U.S. Department of Homeland Security. Retrieved April 1, 2011, from the Web: fema.gov/pdf/about/org/ncp/coop/continuity_plan_template.pdf.

Federal Emergency Management Agency. n.d. *Pandemic Influenza Continuity of Operations Annex Template.* Washington, DC: U.S. Department of Homeland Security. Retrieved April 20, 2011, from the Web: fema.gov/pdf/about/org/ncp/pandemic_influenza.pdf.

Federal Emergency Management Agency. n.d. *Technical Assistance Catalog: Preparedness & Program Management Technical Assistance.* Washington, DC: U.S. Department of Homeland Security. Retrieved April 4, 2011, from the Web: fema.gov/pdf/about/divisions/npd/npd_technical_assistance_catalog.pdf.

Federal Emergency Management Agency. 2004. *Using HAZUS-MH for Risk Assessment: How-To Guide.* Publication Number 433. Washington, DC: U.S. Department of Homeland Security. Retrieved April 4, 2011, from the Web: fema.gov/library/viewRecord.do?id=1985.

Federal Emergency Management Agency. 2007a. Homeland Security Exercise and Evaluation Program (HSEEP), Volumes I–IV. Washington, DC: U.S. Department of Homeland Security. Retrieved April 4, 2011, from the Web: hseep.dhs.gov.

Federal Emergency Management Agency. 2007b. NIMS Compliance Metrics: Terms of Reference. Washington, DC: U.S. Department of Homeland Security. Retrieved April 6, 2011, from the Web: fema.gov/pdf/emergency/nims/comp_met_terms.pdf.

Federal Emergency Management Agency. 2010. *Developing and Maintaining Emergency Operations Plans: Comprehensive Preparedness Guide 101,*

Version 2.0. Washington, DC: U.S. Department of Homeland Security. Retrieved April 4, 2011, from the Web: fema.gov/pdf/about/divisions/npd/CPG_101_V2.pdf.

Federal Emergency Management Agency. 2011a. Hazard Mitigation Planning Resources. Washington, DC: U.S. Department of Homeland Security. Retrieved April 4, 2011, from the Web: fema.gov/plan/mitplanning/resources.shtm.

Federal Emergency Management Agency. 2011b. ICS Resource Center. Washington, DC: U.S. Department of Homeland Security. Retrieved April 6, 2011, from the Web: training.fema.gov/EMIWeb/IS/ICSResource/index.htm.

Federal Emergency Management Agency. 2011c. National Preparedness Directorate: Overview. Washington, DC: U.S. Department of Homeland Security. Retrieved April 4, 2011, from the Web: fema.gov/about/divisions/npd.shtm.

Federal Emergency Management Agency. 2011d. NIMS Resource Center. Washington, DC: U.S. Department of Homeland Security. Retrieved April 4, 2011, from the Web: fema.gov/emergency/nims/.

Federal Emergency Management Agency. 2011e. Plan for Emergencies. Washington, DC: U.S. Department of Homeland Security. Retrieved June 20, 2011, from the Web: fema.gov/plan/prepare/plan.shtm.

Flango, V.E., ed. 2011. *Emergency Preparedness in Dependency Court: Ten Questions That Courts Serving Abused and Neglected Children Must Address.* Williamsburg, VA: National Center for State Courts. Retrieved April 4, 2011, from the Web: icmeducation.org/katrina/.

Hockenberry, S., Sickmund, M., and Sladky, A. 2011. *Juvenile Residential Facility Census, 2008: Selected Findings.* Washington, DC: U.S. Department of Justice, Office of Justice Programs, Office of Juvenile Justice and Delinquency Prevention. Retrieved July 28, 2011, from the Web: www.ncjrs.gov/pdffiles1/ojjdp/231683.pdf.

Interstate Commission for Juveniles. 2011. Lexington, KY: Interstate Commission for Juveniles. Retrieved April 25, 2011, from the Web: www.juvenilecompact.org/home.aspx.

Mankey, J., Baca, P., Rondenell, S., Webb, M., and McHugh, D. 2006. *Guidelines for Juvenile Information Sharing.* Washington, DC: U.S. Department of Justice, Office of Justice Programs, Office of Juvenile Justice and Delinquency Prevention. Retrieved May 10, 2011, from the Web: www.juvenileis.org/pdf/JuvInfoSharing.pdf.

National Center for State Courts. 2007. *Continuity of Court Operations: Steps for COOP Planning.* Williamsburg, VA: National Center for State Courts. Retrieved April 4, 2011, from the Web: contentdm.ncsconline.org/cgi-bin/showfile.exe?CISOROOT=/facilities&CISOPTR=75.

National Child Traumatic Stress Network. 2004. *Trauma-Focused Interventions for Youth in the Juvenile Justice System.* Los Angeles, CA, and Durham, NC: National Child Traumatic Stress Network. Retrieved April 20, 2011, from the Web: nctsnet.org/nctsn_assets/pdfs/edu_materials/trauma_focused_interventions_youth_jjsys.pdf.

National Child Traumatic Stress Network. 2011. Natural Disasters. Los Angeles, CA, and Durham, NC: National Child Traumatic Stress Network. Retrieved April 20, 2011, from the Web: nctsnet.org/trauma-types/natural-disasters.

National Child Traumatic Stress Network and National Center for PTSD. 2006. *Psychological First Aid: Field Operations Guide, 2d Edition.* Los Angeles, CA, Durham, NC, and Washington, DC: National Child Traumatic Stress Network and National Center for PTSD. Retrieved July 27, 2011, from the Web: www.nctsnet.org/sites/default/files/pfa/english/1-psyfirstaid_final_complete_manual.pdf.

National Child Welfare Resource Center for Organizational Improvement. 2007. *Coping with Disasters and Strengthening Systems: A Framework for Child Welfare Agencies.* Washington, DC: U.S. Department of Health and Human Services. Retrieved April 20, 2011, from the Web: muskie.usm.maine.edu/helpkids/rcpdfs/copingwithdisasters.pdf.

National Commission on Children and Disasters. 2009. *Interim Report.* Washington, DC: National Commission on Children and Disasters. Retrieved June 17, 2011, from the Web: cybercemetery.unt.edu/archive/nccd/20110426214349/http://www.childrenanddisasters.acf.hhs.gov/20091014_508IR_partII.pdf.

National Commission on Children and Disasters. 2010. *2010 Report to the President and Congress.* Rockville, MD: Agency for Healthcare Research and Quality. Retrieved June 20, 2011, from the Web: cybercemetery.unt.edu/archive/nccd/20110427002908/http://www.childrenanddisasters.acf.hhs.gov/index.html.

Office of Juvenile Justice and Delinquency Prevention. 2010. National juvenile information sharing initiative. *OJJDP News @ a Glance.* Washington, DC: U.S. Department of Justice, Office of Justice Programs, Office of Juvenile Justice and Delinquency Prevention. Retrieved April 4, 2011, from the Web: ncjrs.gov/html/ojjdp/news_at_glance/230172/sf_6.html.

Office of Juvenile Justice and Delinquency Prevention. 2011. Authorizing Legislation. Washington, DC: U.S. Department of Justice, Office of Justice Programs, Office of Juvenile Justice and Delinquency Prevention. Retrieved April 6, 2011, from the Web: ojjdp.gov/about/legislation.html.

Portune, L., and Gatowski, S.I. 2008. *Ensuring the Unique Needs of Dependency Courts are Met in Disaster Planning Efforts: Dependency Court Planning Templates for Continuity of Operations Plans.* Reno, NV: National Council of Juvenile and Family Court Judges and the American Bar Association. Retrieved April 4, 2011, from the Web: ncjfcj.org/images/stories/dept/ppcd/pdf/katrina%20ta%20brief%20final.pdf.

Qureshi, K., Gebbie, K.M., and Gebbie, E.N. 2006. Job action sheets. In *Implementing ICS within Public Health Agencies.* Public Health Incident Command System, Vol. 1. Retrieved April 6, 2011, from the Web: www.ualbanycphp.org/pinata/phics/guide/phics08.cfm.

Schreiber, M., and Gurwitch, R. 2006. *Listen, Protect, and Connect: Psychological First Aid for Children and Parents.* Los Angeles, CA: University of California Los Angeles, School of Public Health. Retrieved May 11, 2011, from the Web: ready.gov/kids/_downloads/PFA_Parents.pdf.

Substance Abuse and Mental Health Services Administration. 2000. *Psychosocial Issues for Children and Adolescents in Disasters.* Washington, DC: U.S. Department of Health and Human Services. Retrieved April 4, 2011, from the Web: store.samhsa.gov/product/ADM86-1070R.

Substance Abuse and Mental Health Services Administration. 2003. *Mental Health All-Hazards Disaster Planning Guidance.* Washington, DC: U.S. Department of Health and Human Services. Retrieved April 4, 2011, from the Web: store.samhsa.gov/product/SMA03-3829.

Substance Abuse and Mental Health Services Administration. 2009. Crisis Counseling Assistance and Training Program. Washington, DC: U.S. Department of Health and Human Services. Retrieved April 4, 2011, from the Web: store.samhsa.gov/product/SMA09-4373.

Substance Abuse and Mental Health Services Administration. 2011a. Disaster Technical Assistance Center. Washington, DC: U.S. Department of Health and Human Services. Retrieved April 20, 2011, from the Web: samhsa.gov/dtac/.

Substance Abuse and Mental Health Services Administration. 2011b. SAMHSA Disaster Kit. Washington, DC: U.S. Department of Health and Human Services. Retrieved April 4, 2011, from the Web: store.samhsa.gov/product/SMA11-DISASTER.

U.S. Department of Health and Human Services. 2011. Flu.gov. Washington, DC: U.S. Department of Health and Human Services. Retrieved April 21, 2011, from the Web.

Volunteer Management Committee, National Voluntary Organizations Active in Disaster. 2005. *Managing Spontaneous Volunteers in Times of Disaster: The Synergy of Structure and Good Intentions.* Points of Light Foundation, NVOAD, and UPS Foundation. Retrieved May 18, 2011, from the Web: www.citizencorps.gov/downloads/pdf/Managing SpontaneousVolunteers.pdf.

www.ingramcontent.com/pod-product-compliance
Lightning Source LLC
Chambersburg PA
CBHW080908290526
45795CB00007BA/2454